WORDS

&

ART

by

FRANCES
CANNON

GOLD WAKE

the HIGHS & LOWS of SHAPESHIFT MA and BIG-little FRANK

To Mom, obviously.

MOVEMENTS

"By the power of her imagination, this monster had thus been produced..."

On Monsters and Marvels, by Ambroise Pare, 1575

Mom's face mutates in the evening light. Trapped with my mother in a car with a broken radio and no air conditioning, I drift into a state of hallucination. The snake of traffic we have been following down the length of California chokes and bulges as we head into the Bay Area. Mom's nose elongates in the heat waves which drift up from the highway asphalt. Her lips curl into something between a smirk and a grimace in the fumes of passing trucks. The hair on her upper lip—just above that curled smirk—lights up in the glare of sun flashing between planes of metal. She shifts back and forth in my vision between a stunning, tight-skinned, high-cheekboned, golden-haired maiden and a haggard, grey-haired, wrinkled, tattooed witch. Her eyes bulge within their tired sockets, and her jaw takes on an animal sharpness, like the powerful muzzle of a horse.

The human form beside me blends with a vision from my memory: the face of a horse we kept on the family farm in Utah. It's been years since I have even thought of this horse and over a decade since the horse died from binge eating alfalfa. Mom bought this ill-trained Buckskin Arabian on family discount from my great uncle Bob. It was an impulse purchase—not at all practical for a recently-divorced mother of two ornery children and a PhD degree to finish. Perhaps Mom was overcome by a wave of nostalgia, and the horse symbolized a link to her cowgirl childhood, when she rode bareback with her father on the ranch. Or maybe, after being estranged from her family for religious and political differences, she wanted to prove that she still had the skill and courage to tame this rogue mare.

The horse had dun-colored velvet fur, muscles that rippled through her hide, and a matted black mane. I loved her at first sight. I wanted to name her "Mocha," although I was only nine at the time and hadn't yet developed the taste for coffee. I thought the name sounded exotic. Mom had just returned from a research trip in Mexico and wanted to name the horse "Chica." We compromised with "Mochachica."

We soon discovered that our new beloved pet suffered from dangerous behavioral tendencies: biting, kicking, and unexpected galloping. The first time Mom helped me climb onto the horse's back for a little trot, Mochachica immediately kicked her back legs high into the air, sending me flying headfirst over her neck towards a patch of sagebrush. Mom caught me before I split my skull on the hard ground, but I never attempted to ride our horse again. Mochachica also bucked my older sister off within minutes of Eliza's first attempt. My original fascination with this beast was swallowed by fear, and I jumped whenever Mochachica neighed or stomped her massive hooves. Mom was braver, but she gave up after a few months of unsuccessful horse whispering.

Mom asked her sister Ella if we could keep the horse out on the ranch, under Ella's care.

Ella has been nursing a grudge against Mom since Mom left the family farm and left the church. Perhaps Ella viewed Mochachica as a proxy for Mom—both the horse and the woman were stubborn, independent, and feral. Ella let our horse wander away from the other horses, out of sight. Being a horse with a great appetite and little reserve, Mochachica overindulged in alfalfa, bloated, and died alone in a far pasture.

Here, now, in the car on the twilit highway, why do I see Mochachica's veined neck and black sockets lurking beneath Mom's visage? Why do I sense that at any moment, Mom might throw back her mane and neigh out the window at a passing car, or bare her teeth, or shiver the flies from her twitching hide?

I am more than relieved when we finally pull into the hotel parking lot. As a mirage might fade into the shadow of an open road, the horse illusion slips away from Mom's face, and she resumes her human form.

We follow a routine; this hotel is the same as all the others. We've done this before. Mom checks in while I investigate the lobby for free cookies and tea. When we find our room, we kick our shoes across the floor, Mom leaps onto the bed, and I rip the curtains wide open to assess the view or lack-thereof. Mom starts the tap—hot water only—for her ritual bath. She strips down and wanders about the room in the nude while the tub fills up. Her breasts appear round and chipper, even in their frame of fine wrinkles on her chest and hips. She used to tease me for my small, underdeveloped boobs, which she called "mosquito bites" or "kumquats" until my early twenties, when I finally earned her label of "key limes." Mom's chest and forehead are tanned, even sunburned, from our nap on the hood of the car at high noon. Her hair, which reaches halfway down her back, bursts from her scalp in robust waves of deep mahogany, straw, and a hint of white. My hair is short and fuzzy. I trim it myself, every once in awhile, with craft scissors.

To shake off the image of my mother's transmogrified horse-face and the cabin fever I built up during the drive, I leave Mom in the tub and make moves towards my great escape. She calls to me through the crack in the bathroom door, "Are you leaving me?"

"Just exploring, Mom, I'll be back soon," I call back, already closing the door. I wander a few blocks away from our hotel onto the Berkeley campus.

I slip into the old library. I stroke the arm of an old velvet loveseat and admire the paintings in gilded frames which line the walls. One painting in particular draws my attention: a white horse, its jaw and neck contorted in fear, turning to defend itself against the lion on its back, who appears to be biting a chunk out of the horse's spine. I think of the horse of my prior hallucination—Mochachica, the horse-demon of my childhood. Mom's animal spirit seems to contain both the horse's fear and the lion's ferocity, predator and prey, much in the way that the word *passion* contains both fury and panic.

I wander through the aisles, plucking books like ripe fruits to carry under my arm as I browse. It seems to me, in my current state of mind, as though all of these books were written about my mother. I've fled her side but her image pursues me into the psychology section, where I find a book about Jungian dream analysis and a book about the link between creativity and bipolar disorder. I wander through anthropology, and pluck a book about the symbology of ancient myths. What is mother thinking about, alone in the hotel tub. Is she nursing some unpleasant childhood memory like a sore in her cheek? Is she dreaming about finding another mate, to have and to hold, in sickness and in health?

I settle into an ornate chair in the corner under a dim lamp and pick up the book on dream analysis. Mom always appears in my dreams as half-beast, half-human, sometimes a cougar—a sexualized and carnivorous creature. Inspired by the painting on the wall, and mother's earlier transformation in the car, I flip to an entry on horses. The *mother-horse* is a beast of burden, which is gruesome and represents anxiety. Apparently, the horse symbol also led Jung's mind to the libido. I read, "As an animal lower than man the horse represents the *lower part of the body* and the *animal impulses* that rise from there," and I quickly turn the page. I'd rather not linger on the thought of my mother's horse-groin. Or of her breasts, bobbing in the bathwater. Or of that horse-muzzle of rich velvet.

In another book, I look up bipolar disorder, Mom's diagnosis, but here it has another name: "manic depressive insanity." These psychic figures are dual in nature and are prone to "oscillate between their positive and negative meanings." This seems to fit—Mom is always fluctuating between opposites, either unmanageably depressed or frighteningly chipper.

I look up "shape-shifters," and find the archetype of the trickster. This figure has a "dual nature, half animal, half divine," with an "ability to change shape." Appropriate so far, for Mom fluctuates in my gaze as between oracle and beast. As my parent, my mother, she is all-powerful, but as a human, she is fallible. I grin with recognition at the description of this character as a "wounded wounder, an agent of healing." Mom is my troubled caretaker, in need of healing yet also capable of healing me. Maybe I'm the trickster too—doing my best, through my writing, to achieve "transformation of the meaningless into the meaningful." Trying to make sense of the mess of life with my pen.

I am unable to conceptualize my mother as her pure, corporeal self. To me she is more than human. She lingers just below my consciousness throughout each day, a worry-ghost, a shadow of doubt. Or, she hovers above, a talisman of good fortune and wisdom. When I write about her, she transforms. When I dream about her, she transforms. A horse, a mountain lion, a wolf.

This metamorphosis comforts me; my mother becomes a story removed from reality. I more willingly dwell in the realm of myth than confront the raw material of our relationship. She's never merely herself, but a *magical* self. My mother the shapeshifting witch. I pull out my notebook and pen and begin writing a new story,

Ma is up and down, high and low, day in, day out. Sometimes she's up for months at a time and then down for a season. Sometimes she flies and plummets within a single day. She's a shapeshifter, like a man who morphs into a wolf in the poison light of the moon. She's split-brained, like Dr. Jekyll and his unfortunate friend Hyde. Or maybe she's bicephalous, or two-headed, like those baby cows with two heads that scientists keep in jars of formaldehyde or stuff with cotton. Or maybe she's always two different beasts at once, like those mythological creatures with human heads and animal bodies. A centaur. A harpy, with plump, feathered breasts like a fat hen. Or maybe Ma has the head of a beast and a human body, like a Minotaur.

Shapeshift Ma has two daughters: the older one, Eliza, and the younger one, Big-Little Frank. Shapeshift Ma often tells Big-Little Frank how lucky she is for having escaped the family's mental illness. Ma is ill-in-the-head— bipolar— and Frank is ill-in-the-body. When Shapeshift Ma is manic, SHE SPEAKS LIKE THIS. When shape-shift Ma is depressive, *she speaks like this.* Big-Little Frank speaks in a calm, normal tone, because apparently she's the only sane one in the family. She's big and little at the same time because Ma is more of a child than an adult, and Frank often feels like she's her own mother's mother. Big. However, she still feels as pathetic and immature as any other twenty-something she knows—like a child, so she's little at the same time. Big-Little Frank and her wobbly, mentally-ill mother.

Frank imagines Ma as half-pony, walking around town with her human breasts bouncing beneath a long, whiskered muzzle. Ordering coffee through huge horse teeth. Adjusting her dress with human fingers. Whinnying like a wild mare.

Back in the hotel room, I find Mom propped against all of the pillows—including the extras from the closet—watching sitcoms, and all around her are the wadded up wrappers of chocolate.

"Mom, can I write a book about you?"

Mom scratches her bare leg, which protrudes akimbo from her hotel bathrobe. Her fingernails are much too long—from negligence, not from fashion. The sound of these nails against her dry skin and thick black leg stubble gives me a lemon-pucker-face. She doesn't respond to my question, so I continue,

"In the piece I've started writing you're a horse. Is that ok?"

She frowns. Scratches her leg.

"A whore? I'm not sure; that's a bit harsh, don't you think? I mean sure, I'm sexually active, but a whore? Is that what you think about me?"

"No, not a whore, a horse! The animal! In the story I mean."

Mom shrugs, and she clears away the candy wrappers so that I may snuggle in next to her on the bed. She's still scratching her leg hairs, and I'm tempted to swat her hand away, but I've tried that before—unsuccessfully. She'll just keep scratching. My mother. I wonder what shape she will take tonight. Horse? Wolf? Woman? And I—will I be old? Young? A grandmother? A two-headed androgynous cherub? A rabbit?

the EMBRYO

In the beginning, Big-Little Frank and Shapeshift Ma are entwined in a safe, warm egg. They are whole and contained in one another's company. They are self-sufficient, unaware of the noises and activity outside of their egg. The egg is their relationship, and nothing exists outside of this. Ma is great. Ma is the Good Mother. She has dangling, milk-filled breasts and a body of generous flesh to hug and to hold. She is faceless—just a soft mass of comfort. Big-Little Frank is simple and small for now. She is the budding protagonist of this tale, but only now a sprout of what she shall become.

*

It runs in the family, this tendency towards up-and-down, high-and-low instability, along with a whole varietal bouquet of depression and anxiety. Shape-shift Ma is always eager to ramble off the names of our relatives with mental illness, as though she were bragging about a superhuman power passed down from generation to generation. Or maybe she takes comfort that they're all trapped in the same boat—that she's not floating out alone in the waters of depression.

There's grandma Jean, for example, recently dead. She kept pamphlets around the house with titles like "Ten Ways to Prepare for Your Own Death." For over a decade, she said her ankles hurt too much to walk around, but the family knew she was just too sad to leave her living room.

There's aunt Betty, whose hair fell out from too much worrying, so now she has to wear a wig that doesn't match her eyebrows. She never leaves her house. She hasn't had a job or an independent project since she had her first kid, and now the grandkids leave little time for a change of lifestyle. Fulfilling the Mormon family ideal: go forth and propagate, then stay at home.

Aunt Mandy occasionally forgets her identity and wanders like an orphan or a ghost around the produce section of Walmart, calling out for God. Fortunately, she lives in a small town, and everyone knows about her lapses of memory and perpetual disorientation.

They drive her home, pat her on the shoulder and say, "See you in church, Mandy. Take Care."

There's aunt Ella, who has burrowed so fervently into her little Mormon cave of conservative politics and judgement that she won't even answer the phone.

Since she took over the family ranch, she rips garlic bulbs from thick slabs of clay in the far field and combs her children's hair in rough, decisive strokes from the top of the scalp down. She thinks Ma is the Devil's mistress for all her sins: leaving the Church, divorcing husband #1, drinking alcohol, sleeping around, drinking coffee, divorcing husband #2, befriending homosexuals and liberals, the list goes on. Ella sends Ma letters calling her the "Devil's whore" and by extension her children are the "Devil's spawn." She burns the letters that Ma sends in the wood stove.

Everyone in the family is addicted to sugar, especially uncle Peter with the potbelly and a bad case of pessimism. He's tried everything from yoga to basketball in order to cure his depression, but then he gives up, which drives him to eat more sugar, which makes him fat, which makes him sad, which drives him to eat more sugar.

Then there's Shapeshift Ma, of course. She's the youngest of the six children. Left home at sixteen to pursue multiple degrees: journalism, anthropology, sociology. Married an engineer. Left the church. Had two daughters, including Big-Little Frank. Had an affair with the next door neighbor. Divorced the engineer. Started moving around the country. Published five academic books on polygamy. Teaches courses on gender, social deviance, and family structure. Married a Native American landscape artist. Divorced him after he slept with a younger woman. Now working on a novel about a woman who runs away from her polygamous family to pursue a romantic relationship with her sister-wife. She's hard to keep track of, even for her daughters.

Ma's two faces are dangerously day and night. When she's day, she spends all her money at once and moves across the country for no reason but a change of scenery. When she's night, she weeps and clings to her children's cheeks as though fingers to flesh will keep her from dissolving into the ether.

Frank doesn't agree when Ma tells her that Frank's the only sane one. Ma doesn't know what kind of weird stuff goes on behind Frank's Big-Little face, and if Ma did know, she would stop congratulating Frank on her good fortune, because then Frank would be the most ill of all. She would be ill-in-the-head *and* ill-in-the-body. Tough luck. If only Ma knew.

*

Frank was big even when she was really little. When she was small enough to fit with her legs folded in a pretzel shape in her mother's lap, she knew about trouble and sadness. She understood—in the way one understands gravity before one has a word for it— about sex, arguments, affairs, loss of faith, pain.

At this age, Frank's hair had not fully grown in and was concentrated in one soft, blond tuft on the top of her head that swirled back like soft serve ice cream flicked by a tongue. She kept herself busy drawing princesses and toads and hoarding Halloween candy in pillowcases under her mattress until ant colonies discovered her cache of sweets.

She didn't always have the words to describe her dark observations to Eliza, so she kept them secret. When she did share her dark thoughts, her sister would stare back with eyes as wide and white as gumballs. She once asked Eliza, "Do you know what Mom and Dad do at night that makes so much noise, like they're moving furniture around for hours and hours?" Eliza gave her the gumball stare.

Sometimes Frank whispers her own secrets to Big Daddy, the life-sized stuffed bear that lives in her bed. Big Daddy is her most trusty confidant, until she comes home one day from preschool to find Big Daddy's legs dangling out of the trash can on the curb and cotton oozing from a ripped stitch in his face. Her Dad says he threw the bear away "because Big Daddy was infested with ants." Frank is more hesitant to share her thoughts with anyone after Big Daddy's disappearance.

One of Frank's first memories, from around age four or five, is finding Ma's divorce papers on the kitchen table. She asked Ma about them, and Ma's expression told Frank a whole, silent story—a story about how strange and hard life would be from that moment on and about how Ma wasn't hurt as much as guilty and confused. Like when their dog knocked over the trash or peed on the carpet—Dad would yell and yell in the dog's face, but all he got in response was that expression of guilt and confusion. That was the face Ma revealed to Frank, and Frank grew big real quick, right then. She didn't know about divorce or alimony or custody or adultery, but she knew that these papers were dangerous and that her mother had done something much worse than knocking over the trash or peeing on the carpet.

*

When Ma is manic, the world moves too slowly. She tries to speed it up by dancing in circles around everyone who crosses her path: her husband, her children, her employers. Once, Ma and Frank were on a road trip, and Ma pointed out the car window to a tunnel of red dust in a nearby field. "That's called a dust devil," she told Frank, and then without warning, she pulled their car off the road, through the gutter, and straight into the field to chase the spinning tower of dirt. They chased the dust devil across a crop of young corn until it dissipated in the wind.

Ma's like that dust devil—she sucks her loved ones up into the turbulence of her enthusiasm. This process can be exhilarating for her audience, because when Ma is up she is up and fun and hot and high and her laugh fills the room and she dances on tabletops and paints canvases with vibrant oils and kisses strangers. But sometimes she spins too fast, and Frank gets dizzy trying to hold on.

When Ma's manic, she makes decisions for the sake of novelty, for spontaneous adventure. One could say that in these times she is impulsive, even rash—but she doesn't see it this way in the moment. She is wild and fun, like a young mare running free and naked through a meadow of sunflowers with her mane flitting to and fro in the breeze. In these upswings, she has so much love to give that she can't fit her affection into standard boxes like marriage or other stuffy social contracts. Blood boils hot in her loins, and she wants to chase down men as though they were feral mustangs that she can break and ride one by one with her beauty and charm.

So it is when Ma is up. When she's down, she gets down low enough to win any limbo contest around. Look at her go, bending backwards, walking the squat under that limbo pole. Look how close she gets to scraping her skull on the ground when she bends down so low. In this position, she tends to make quick decisions, just like in her upswings, but these are different. She quits jobs. She quits cities. She picks up and moves on. "Scratch that, start fresh," she seems to say. She swipes her hand across the table of her life, clearing her view of clutter, sending cups and saucers, loved ones and homes, crashing to the floor. Or, she smashes the table. Tears up the house. She is her own demolition crew, a deconstructor. She builds homes here and there and then runs in with her hammer and tears down the rafters.

Frank has many jumbled images of this hammer-wielding Ma, here, there, tearing, building, deconstructing, constructing, moving, bouncing, traveling. It's hard to keep the logistics of it all straight. How old was Frank when Ma first left Salt Lake City for Santa Cruz, and how old was she when Ma moved back? How many houses in Utah did they occupy, how many neighborhoods, how many schools? Did they move to Maine or Oregon first? Montana or Vermont first?

Frank doesn't have enough fingers and toes to count out all the times she has moved, or the houses she has lived in. When anyone asks, "Where are you from?" she either picks a city randomly out of the bunch, or she offers a shrug of the shoulders and the open palms of unknowing. "Maybe... Utah? I've spent the most time in Oregon, California, and Vermont, so maybe one of those..." When people ask the more sticky question, "Why?" Frank offers the same shrug and open palms, and as though it were a nervous tick, she spins her pointer finger in the space beside her ear: the universal sign for insanity, and states matter-of-factly "crazy Mom."

Ma has always been handy. She grew up in a dirt-poor family in boondock hicksville desert town in Utah. Not that there are any hicks in Ma's family: they read and play the cello and sing and write and teach and all the other signifiers of intelligence and creativity, blah blah blah. Above all else, though, the family has a sturdy work ethic. A do-it-yourself Macgyver meets Swiss Family Robinson type attitude. If the irrigation pipes break, all the kids run out in the frosted pre-dawn fields to haul the heavy metal around, stumbling over frozen ditches in their slippers. Ma still carries this kick-ass cowgirl carpenter spirit around, even though now she's a city-dwelling professor. She buys houses, tears them down, rebuilds them with her own two hands, and puts them back on the market. This would be a very wise financial scheme except that Ma can't sit still, so she often moves before the house is done or is forced to sell when the market's low because she just can't wait. Can't wait, she's late! Late for what, Frank will never know. Late to catch up with her up. She's either up and chasing adventure or down and fleeing the shadow-fingers of a sourceless grief.

The girls were never able to settle into any one house before they were back on the road. They may have spent more time growing up in cars, motels, and tents than in houses. Every few seasons, Ma announced that it was time for a new road trip. She turned these trips into games. She would start these road trips off with a three-part ritual. A holy trinity of road trip habits. First, she would accelerate and raise her free arm into the wind. Then, she would shout "We could go all the way to Mexico!" Finally, she would sing the first few phrases of Willie Nelson's "On the Road Again," either until she forgot the lyrics or lost interest.

Frank grew familiar with the props of this travel drama. She knows the stiff linen pulled painfully tight around the mattress, the hay-tinted polyester throw blanket that inevitably slips onto the floor in the middle of the night, the pillows that collapse into two dimensions upon impact, the hum of the radiator by the window that lulls her into a daze, the forced intimacy of limited space. She knew the false moon glow of the streetlamp through the thin curtain. Ma trained the girls to hoard soaps and towels. They would patter in complimentary slippers through lobbies carrying Styrofoam plates of stale English muffins for road snacks. Ma would stuff the empty spaces of her purse, her coat pockets, and her suitcase with packets of instant coffee, creamers, and miniature bottles of lotion. Despite the redundancy of these accumulated nights, she pranced about with the same pony glee from one Days Inn to the next Motel 6 as though she had tapped into the essence of novelty.

Early on, Frank tries to reconstruct the egg-womb of her innocent child-self. One cannot rebuild an egg, however. All the king's horses and all the king's men cannot put Frank's egg together again. So, Frank begins building instead her own inner mobile home: a structure inside herself where she could hide out from intruders, or curl up with a storybook and cup of hot chocolate. She builds walls to keep herself upright and to keep certain people and things out. Every time the family moves, which is nearly every year, she has to start over, nailing boards to her inner house. She reinforces a rafter here, adds a column there. Just building her house, nothing to see here. Don't look inside, there's nothing to see. Just a nice, sturdy little house. Every once in a while, Ma takes her hammer and tears down Frank's house. Frank has no foundation, no protection, no more walls. Ma breaks the dam and Frank comes pouring out. Ma breaks the egg, and the yolk spills out.

My mother wriggles like a fish when she hears the words "complimentary breakfast." On road trips, she wraps motel rolls of bread in napkins and stuff them guiltily, hurriedly into her purse. She slips handfuls of butter pads, instant coffee, and an assortment of jellies and spreads into the pocket of her coat.

My mother's wardrobe is also a clear reflection of her frugality. I doubt that she has ever in her adult life purchased a new, full priced item of clothing, except underwear. She is a walking advertisement for the Salvation Army, although nothing ever really fits and she could care less about matching colors. The items that she can't find in a secondhand store, such as lipstick, socks, or groceries, she finds in dollar stores and warehouses for damaged goods. When she runs out of hygiene items such as razors or shampoo, she simply abstains until they go on sale. It is for this reason that she shaves her legs only once a month, and that her socks are all worn down at the heel and toe area. She cuts corners as much as possible when it comes to bills and lifestyle expenses. She keeps the house at 50 degrees, even in the heart of bitter winters, and she chastises us for taking long showers or for flushing when it is not necessary. When she takes baths, she fills the tub only five inches with water.

I can't write my mother off as merely frugal: she goes beyond thrift into a state of mania, in which she twists the world like a wet sponge for any moisture that may have been denied her in her youth. She justifies these behaviors with an invisible scale of balance. If she spends money, she should be amply compensated. Therefore, when something goes wrong, such as a cancelled flight, or a bump in the night during her peaceful hotel stay, she brings out her weapon of complaint. Often her efforts reward her with extra pillows, meal tickets, monetary reimbursement, or free beverages. She waves these rewards like flags, as proof of her wisdom to her skeptical family. Sometimes, however, her imagined scale leads her to troublesome reasoning. If a doctor, chiropractor, or dentist cannot swiftly and painlessly cure her ailments, she tells me that "these good-for-nothing doctors spend so much time on their lunch breaks that they can't fit any time in for research. The whole system is corrupted. Overpaid ignorance." As she is against spending money to support such corrupt institutions as hospitals and banks, she often refuses to comply with mainstream practices. She will only take her daughters or herself to the hospital if the injury in question was fatal.

*

Frank is eight or so, running barefoot through the yard in the avenues of Salt Lake. Ma is fixing up this house so she can flip it back on the market. She's inside knocking down a wall with a hammer. Frank hops on a broken beer bottle with her foot. The glass slices upwards between her veins. She howls so loud a squirrel falls out of a nearby tree. She drenches the sidewalk in her blood. After she pulls the glass out and stumbles up the stairs of the house, screaming, Ma washes her foot with iodine, wraps it in a thick bandage, puts Frank on the couch with a popsicle, and tells Frank to watch a movie, *Harold and Maude*, until she falls asleep. Ma never takes Frank to see a doctor, and her foot soon becomes infected. It smells like old chicken and mushroom soup from a can. She has to hop on one leg for over a month since Ma can't find reasonably priced secondhand crutches.

Mom has always been sensitive about vacations. She doesn't like to share her daughters with her ex-husband. One day the three of us—Mom and us girls—are on a hike, chittering and chattering about boys and school and jobs, when out of the blue Mom brings up the subject of Christmas. She offers to take the us to Paris, or Scotland, or some such extravagant and impulsive holiday. I hesitate and suggest that to be fair, "We should ask Dad what he has in mind." Apparently, this translates poorly to Mom, who begins to whine,

"It's not fair! You don't love me! You've never loved me as much as I love you! You obviously don't want to spend Christmas with me, I can tell by your expression. That's fine, I know you love your father more. They have more money and you'll probably have more fun in Portland. Enjoy it. I just miss you guys so much when you're away."

Eliza consoles Mom in the best way she knows how: to sob along with her. I become real quiet, leaning away from the conversation. I don't want to be sucked into their whirlpool. I don't have the energy to cry and throw a fit. I'd rather stay in my own head, so I redirect my full attention to popping the heads off Black-Eyed Susan flowers that line the path. I'm building myself a little cabin, inside of myself, to take shelter from the winds that Mom and Eliza are kicking up. I tune out the noise of their bickering and occupy myself with the weeds. Mom turns her attention to my silence and blubbers,

"You're not even listening! You don't care! I love you and you could care less! Can't you see how upset I am? Do you have any empathy? Do you have intimacy problems? Are you heartless? Have I made a cold-blooded monster of my own daughter?"

*

Perhaps Ma made a monster of Frank, as she suggests. This either means that they are both monsters, together, or that Ma created a new monster in the form of a daughter. Is Frank becoming Ma due to inevitable genetic inheritance? Or, perhaps, Frank's present anxieties and neurotic behaviors stem from an inter-generational epigenetic trauma—either trauma which Ma experienced as a child and passed on to Frank or the trauma of Frank's own bizarre childhood.

Ma says Frank is "cold-blooded." Like a lizard or a dragon. The ancients wrote of mothers who accidentally birthed monsters through the power of their imaginations. Aristotle, Hippocrates, Empedocles, and Ambroise Paré—scientists of the old world—wrote of mothers who looked too long at a profane painting and thereby produced a hermaphrodite or a double-headed cow-child in their womb. Specifically, Ambroise Paré wrote in his 1575 bestiary *On Monsters and Marvels* about the process by which a monster is created in the mother's mind; the mother's twisted psychic visions manifest themselves in her womb. A monster forms in the "ardent and obstinate imagination that the mother might receive at the moment she conceived—through some fantastic dream—of certain nocturnal vision that the man or woman have at the hour of conception."

So Ma created in Frank the shapeshifting monster in the imaginative hour of sex. Baby Frank grew in Ma's womb, already an old woman in a little girl's body, with a lizard heart, who sometimes takes the shape of a rabbit.

the SPLIT

A small crack appears in the shell of the egg. Egg white oozes out through the split in the shell. Where the white escapes, light filters in. The light wakes Ma and Frank out of their nap. Frank recognizes that something is wrong—Ma is not a simple, whole, normal mother; she is of a dual nature. They fidget, they shift, they poke one another in the belly with their sharp elbows. They are still entwined, but they are very uncomfortable. It's too tight in here. They can't breathe. They start to sense their egg-cabin-fever. Frank is aware, for the first time, that this intimacy is strange—she is much too old to be hugging her naked mother in an egg. She must get out. Ma has her own ideas, Frank has her doubts, and they begin to bicker. Slowly at first, but soon the noise of their bickering creates more cracks in the egg's shell. The shell eventually collapses and Ma and Frank, like one sloppy, fragile yolk, spill out into the open air.

Ma meets a handsome Native American artist on a trip through Montana. They marry a few months after their first date, and James soon moves in with us. After their marriage, Ma can't seem to contain her giddiness. She wins at life! Sometimes she calls herself a pony and prances one, two, three, four times around the kitchen island. Everyone in the family laughs, but for different reasons. Ma laughs because she is imitating a pony. Frank laughs because she feels as though she is watching a comedy skit about a dysfunctional family on television or a psychological study about a woman regressing back to her cowgirl childhood. Eliza laughs because she and Ma are kindred spirits. James laughs to humor Ma, in order to avoid another of her daily mental breakdowns. He is a good support: when she gets low and sobs, he holds her silently, listens, nodding. Ma the pony doesn't see what's coming.

*

Halfway through their marriage, Mom and James decide to try to expand their marriage into an unconventional long-distance experiment. James moves to Montana, where he feels closer to the land, more in tune with the quiet spirit of nature. He also has more clientele for his wilderness paintings in the Wild West. Mom stays in Vermont where she is a tenured Anthropology professor. This seems strange at me at first, but the idea grows on me. They seem just as much in love, and in a way, the odd model looks and feels healthier than being stuck in the same house day in, and day out. This works well enough for a few years, until Mom's house burns down. We're still not quite sure how it happened. The insurance company finally claims "accident without apparent origin," and once again, Mom begins her frantic cycle of hopping from one house to the next. Both Eliza and I finally leave the house for college, and Mom sinks into a heavy empty-nesting depression. We have no home base, really, only a tenuous web of residences.

"At least I still have a home in James's arms," she sighs to me on the phone.

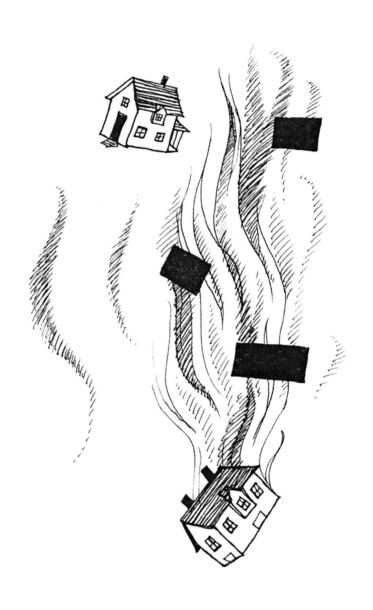

*

Ma's mother Jean gets pancreatic cancer around Christmas. We all travel to Utah to tend to Jean on her hospice cot. And Ma, in her ever-precarious state, slaves away in the kitchen preparing a Christmas Eve feast.

James takes Frank outside before dinner to tell her a secret, of sorts. Fourteen years into his marriage with Ma, James wants to ask for a divorce. He is recruiting Frank to help him make the big announcement. He needs Frank to be ready with open arms to pick up the pieces of any potential explosion, to sweep up his mess, to catch Ma if she leaps off the edge.

All rudimentary architecture that Frank has built inside herself since the house fire returns to a state of flame. Everything burns. What a perfect holiday gift. How convenient of James to ask for a divorce while Ma's mother wastes away on a hospice cot. And Ma, in her ever-precarious state, all the more fragile after the fire. Frank wants to demand, "why now? Why do I have to help Mom, and not my older sister Eliza? What did Mom do wrong?" But she keeps her questions to herself, for she knows she has no choice. Who else can rescue Ma?

James decides that it's best to spring the news right away, before he loses his nerve. He sends Frank in on her own, because he doesn't want to "upset Jean" on her deathbed. Frank floats into the house, herald of destruction. There's Ma, wearing an apron and holding a pan of roasted chicken at breast height, grinning behind the counter like a 1950's advertisement for kitchen equipment. Jean and Eliza are at the table, playing dominoes and drinking tall glasses of grape juice. Frank feels light-headed as she drifts into Ma's arms like a ghost, biting her tongue until it bleeds to keep from crying. Ma whispers into Frank's hair,

"Finally! Together for Christmas, all of us here, isn't it wonderful?"

Frank practically vomits tears into Ma's sweater. Strings of saliva cling to Ma's shoulder as Frank pulls away, but she puts on a poker face and says what James told her to say, like a good puppet.

"Mom, let's all go on a little walk to work up an appetite before dinner. James is outside, he wants to stretch his legs." She spits these words out and immediately wants to purge this afternoon's soup all over her grandmother's carpet.

They all head out towards the hill above Jean's house, except Jean of course, who hasn't moved much beyond her La-Z-Boy chair in months. Frank feels complicit in a lie rotten enough to curdle milk. She feels just that—rotten, as though a bloom of mold has grown a fat mushroom in her abdomen. She hates

James for asking her to help him. Eliza has no clue. Ma has no clue. They stroll along the pathway leading up to the cemetery, where Ma likes to hike for a view of the Salt Lake City valley. She calls this "bunny hill" because wild rabbits have taken over the cemetery as a breeding ground. The bunnies proliferate in and around the gravestones all along the walk, and every time one pops out of a bush, Ma giggles and points like a kindergartner at the zoo. How the hell is Frank supposed to react: laugh along? Ignore Ma? Scream like a banshee and hurl curses at James for putting her in such an awkward position? She turns her face into the bushes, away from Ma's gaze, as the family mounts the hill and approaches the edge of the cliff.

They pause here to take in the view from the precipice: Salt Lake City's urban and suburban sprawl illuminates every millimeter of the once barren and wild valley with artificial light. Only a decade ago, Frank romped as a child in the foothills of these Wasatch mountains, gathering watercress from pristine creeks and scouting for horny toad lizards. Now a perpetual swath of pink smog clings like phlegm or like rolls of fat flesh to the city. Ma doesn't seem to notice the smog. She sucks in breath through a grin and gathers her daughters and husband into a hug, mumbling "Together, finally, for the holidays." What sick joke is this? Frank feels her saliva strings beginning to form to Ma's hair again, as though she were some slug that leaves a trail of snot on everyone she touches.

Here in this embrace, Frank feels James's enormous arms tightening around the ladies. He's a strong man. A strong, scary-looking man with biceps thicker than both of Frank's thighs and neck veins that pop when he clenches his jaw. Frank was scared shitless of James when Ma first married him—who was this giant Native American pulling into the driveway on his Harley Davidson, with more scars than she could count and a nose crooked from so many punches?

James's hug grip begins to frighten Frank, and she thinks of the rabbits in the shadows, their little hearts beating with fear. Just as Frank begins to push against this claustrophobic trap, James clears his throat. Here it goes. Frank goes limp but nobody notices because they're all so tightly packed. She wants out. She's through being James's conspirator. This is fucked up. She tunes out to James's announcement. Divorce. Frank's already seen this, Ma's already been through this. She pants—a trapped rabbit—as James mumbles his proclamation. He has to say it five times, five different ways, before Ma begin to understand what's happening. The speech is lost to Frank except the single phrase, which James repeats over and over and over again, until his voice cracks and dissolves into a hoarse whisper,

"I just can't do it, I can't do it anymore, I can't, I can't do this, I can't do it. I just can't do it...."

Now it's Ma's turn to transfigure into a rabid beast, a wild mare—slobbering, frothing at the mouth, neighing, thrashing her mane about. She approaches the cliff and suddenly it hits Frank that she might actually leap off. This is why James asked for her help—Ma's daughters are emotional anchors to keep her from hurling herself into the Salt Lake smog. Three sets of hands grab at Ma, and it takes three bodies to wrestle her away from the edge. They lock her in an embrace, if you could call it that. More like a human straightjacket. Ma pushes against Frank's grip with such vehemence that Frank fears Ma's condemnation: this is Frank's fault for playing along with James's twisted game. Ma hates Frank. There's nothing Frank can do to keep Ma from leaping off this cliff.

Frank glances to James and sees in his eyes the plea of a stupid child. He can't save Ma. She glances to Eliza, who is lost in her own mess of sobs— she can't save Ma. So Frank steels herself, sheds her rabbit quiverings, and grabs Ma's face with both hands, close to her own, so that there is only an inch between their dripping noses.

*

The timing is cosmitragic. Grandma Jean leaves the realm of flesh not long after James picks up and leaves, lickety-split. Eliza returns to her job and boyfriend in Vermont. At Jean's funeral, Ma and Frank are the only ones in the family willing to sort through the junk in the abandoned bedroom. Perhaps her siblings are afraid of encountering their mother's ghost, so freshly departed. Or perhaps they are reluctant to handle Jean's used tissues and incontinence diapers. In any case, Frank lingers around the bookshelves, nervously transferring mystery novels into boxes, and brave Ma takes charge of the bedroom. In her sweep, Ma discovers Jean's beloved Bible, tucked under the pillow. The book has gold-tinged pages thin as butterfly wings bound in well-worn cowhide. Ma rubs her finger along the edge of the pages as she flutters them rhythmically back and forth, back and forth, generating a gentle wind on her chin. Ma does this with all of her books when she loses herself in thought—flipping the corner of her mystery novels while staring off into space. She mimics the gesture with Slinkies, which she keeps in every drawer in the house. They calm her, these little metal spring toys of yore. She rubs them in between her finger, worrying, smoothing, meditating. While flipping the gilded pages of her deceased mother's Bible, a small slip of paper falls out onto the bedsheets. The paper holds a quote in Jean's fragile handwriting—handwriting carrying the pain of illness and nostalgia:

"The test of a first-rate intelligence is the ability to hold two opposed ideas in the mind at the same time, and still retain the ability to function."
— Francis Scott Fitzgerald, *The Crack-up*

Ma shares the note with Frank, and Frank tastes synchronicity. Has Jean's spirit reached back into the realm of flesh to scribble one last quote for Ma and Frank?

*

Big-Little Frank decides to distract Ma from her utter despair after James's untimely announcement and Jean's funeral by stealing Ma away on a summer-long, cross-country road trip. Frank can see that if she leaves Ma alone, Ma will split in half, or spontaneously combust. She can hear it in Ma's staccato voice when she says,

"I just don't understand what went wrong...and why everything has to happen all at once..."

They drive from Utah through Idaho, Oregon, Washington, Montana, Wyoming, South Dakota, and Iowa. They pretend to hike, but mostly they bicker. Bicker, bicker, bicker, as though they are developing a new language—a very clipped language sprinkled with expletives. A language that, if drawn on a piece of paper, might resemble the line of a seismograph or heart monitor: up, down, up, down. Silence, outburst, silence, outburst. Peaks of great volume chopped by overdrawn lulls. Excessively stressed syllables.

"MA! Do you have to cry here? Now? In public? Can we talk about this later?"

"You'll never love me as much as I love you, I'VE RUINED YOU, I've made you hard and cold, I'm such a bad mother..."

Ma and Frank pull into a rest stop in South Dakota to address a number of near-emergency needs: both of their bladders verge on bursting, their water bottles have been sucked dry, and they have reached the conclusions of three books on tape. Frank awkwardly pisses into a stainless steel urinal, since the women's bathroom is occupied by a dozen greying lady geese. Ma stocks up on free donuts and coffee while Frank tries to piece together a highway trajectory from four different tourist brochures. They manage to navigate to a backroads pond before the sun sets on the cliffs of the Badlands.

Ma refuses to pay the ten-dollar entrance fee to the national park campground, so they drive a few hours off-route on dirt roads to a mud pond in the middle of bumfuck nowheresville to set up camp. When they arrive, Ma grumbles, "Mosquitropolis," and Frank thinks, "There goes any chance of enjoying the wilderness."

They haven't activated their bum muscles since sunrise, so they agree to embark on an evening walk-about. The hike through marshes and climb barbed wire fences in pursuit of the setting sun, the mysterious geological cliffs, and the pelicans on the opposite side of the pond.

Ma and Frank come to the edge of a bog, and Ma hesitates, "Why don't we turn back and set up camp?" But Frank is stubborn. She must walk into the sunset. She must walk until she sweats out the toxins of ennui that built up in her lymph nodes during the dozens of hours in the car. So, they hoist their skirts and trudge through the duck sludge, which rises with wet mystery to their thigh flesh. Ma wipes the green-brown-grey ooze—a cocktail of waterfowl excrement and farm runoff—from her skin with stiff weeds. They help each other climb through, over, and under several barbed wire fences. "Nearly to the edge of the cliff," Frank insists, although the rock formation seems to recede with every step, it shimmers in a mirage of evening sunlight. When they finally reach the cliff, they find that the grand view they had been pursuing all along contained an abandoned village of defunct tractors. A wilderness of South Dakota trash. Neither Ma nor Frank says a word on the long trek back to the tent. Ma loses a shoe in the bog.

As they mount the last hillock, their heavy steps disturb a squadron of pelicans who lift one-by-one into the air. Without having to speak, the minds of Ma and Frank merge. Their synchronized thoughts turn the slow, awkward pelicans into pterodactyls. Prehistoric lizard-birds. The long walk to the cliff, the fences, the lost shoe, these worries fall into the grass as mother and daughter observe the beauty of dusk in the Badlands. They walk hand-in-hand to their car, where they each crack a beer. Ma offers Frank a peach, and they both laugh as peach juice runs down Frank's chin. They fall asleep curled together on a quilt in the grass, half-drunk from dehydration and lukewarm pale ale. Frank loves her mother, fully, until the mosquitoes start to bite and Ma leaps up to pace around the car, fretting and moaning and swatting at the bugs until sunrise. Then Frank loves Ma just a little less.

When Frank turns twenty-five and Ma turns fifty, they begin to merge. Frank becomes the mom, and Ma becomes the kid. They both go crazy. Frank grows up much too quickly, and Ma unravels into teenagedom. In the process of switching roles, they temporarily melt into the same being, sharing many of the same quirky traits and overlapping in odd, eerie ways. They both come of age, together, simultaneously. They're both single and juggling lovers, though Mom's lovers are dudes and Frank's are gay women or genderqueer humans. Little Frank gets an adult job in academia, just like her old Ma; she moves to Iowa to pursue a graduate degree and gets hired as an assistant professor of literature. Ma gets really hot: slim, trim, tan, while Frank starts to age in all the wrong places: wrinkled, knobby-kneed, arthritic, bruised. Ma starts drinking and smoking pot and is really FUN !*$!*!#!$!. She has a lot of sex while Frank has very little. During her time in Iowa, Frank goes through more periods of sadness, while Ma starts to act really happy, but Frank worries that this guise of cheer is just a precarious, extended manic state. Ma might plummet at any moment, and Frank stands by with her net.

Mom inundates me with emails, phone calls, and the occasional handwritten, snail mail letter, written on flowery stationary that she steals from her roommate's stationery cabinet. Such as this letter, which I receive soon after my move to Iowa.

Sweet Francie,

I'm impressed at how quickly you adapt to new environments! I'm jealous of your perpetual happiness. You seem to be the only stable one in the family, the only person to have escaped mental illness. You're so lucky to be so happy all the time, you make life look so easy! I'm secretly waiting for the day when your dark Bennion blood rises to the skin, but maybe you've escaped all that. I'm so proud of you. Keep it up, sweetie!

Love, your Momma

Mom also sends me daily text message updates about her romantic and sexual exploits, as well as frequent selfies, always with the same pursed-lipped, "come hither" facial expression, with backdrops of mountain peaks, bridges over idyllic streams, or fields of wheat, where she stands wearing tight dresses and too much makeup. I can't keep all the men in the texts straight.

"I'm dining w a man w the perfect qualities I seek except he's not kissable."

A month passes, and she's texting about a new guy.

"I'm bonkers for this dude. He is an engineer and a pilot and a sweet and kind man. I may be in trouble here. My heart is beginning to ache. Advice? Buddhist detachment is not working."

Another month passes, and she's head over heels with someone new.

"I'm making pot butter for my date tonight!"

And again...

"I have a new friend who went hiking with me yesterday to the waterfall. He's from a ranching family and is a Delta pilot who has his own money (that's a plus!) I like him and he is a good man."

And again...

"New beau! 38 year old Belgian anthropologist. Nice kisser, great conversationalist. Why he likes me, I'll never know."

I most often ignore the texts, but I'll respond when I sense a need to intervene, to slow the pace of Mom's explosive and ever-expanding sexual exploits. When Mom travels back to Montana to sell her house—the house in which James cheated on Mom with their hot young neighbor—she sends me notifications about her new dates. I find it disturbing that she feels the need to sleep around on the stomping grounds of her fresh divorce, but I respond with vaguely positive affirmations like "cool," or "glad you're enjoying yourself." When she tells me that she is planning to bring a new fellow—a pilot or a lawyer or someone equally dull and professional—to James's art exhibit, I break our chain of emojis with this:

"Mom, do you really think it's a good idea to bring your new OkCupid date to your ex-husband's art show? You've only just finalized the divorce! Maybe you are both a little too fragile for this type of interaction. Maybe Mr. Daniel is oblivious to the drama, but he'll likely catch on after a few minutes. Are you doing this to get back at James for cheating on you with a younger woman? Yes, he may be jealous and uncomfortable, but I think a better lesson would be to prove to James that you are capable of living a fulfilling, happy life independently. Give yourself some breathing room. It's too soon for revenge. Also, even though I haven't met him, I had a dream that you married Mr. Daniel for his money and the wedding party consisted of excessive amounts of champagne, widescreen televisions, and over-chlorinated hot tubs. Not a good scene. Love you, but take care of yourself."

Triple clap of thunder in my attic bedroom. A vase of flowers rattles with the force of sound. The thunder rouses me from a jumble of uncomfortable dreams about Mom—homelessness, vagrancy, running from murderous tigers, fighting about bills. My dreams often play out in fragments, like short films or the multiple acts of a play. Though it is still dark out, I can't get back to sleep—the sheets seem stained with nightmare sweat. Instead, I flip on a lamp and scribble out what I can remember from tonight's dream, before the thunder interrupted.

At first, the two of us are homeless, on the move. We only have a few possessions: one wooden bench, on which we sleep, sit, and eat. Sometimes we turn the bench upside-down like a sled to travel down hill slopes. I carry all of my possessions on my back: my letters, my books, and my artwork. I tell Mom to guard my pile while I try to steal a loaf of bread from the grocery store, but Mom leaves my things in the rain. Everything is ruined.

The landscape shifts, and my dreamself shrinks backwards in time. I'm smaller, younger, more fragile. I find Mom in the bathtub. A young man with long hair sits on the toilet. On the floor lie dozens of needles. Mom's face is submerged in tub water. Her limbs are blue. Motionless. I begin howling questions at the man while I struggle to lift her slippery, water-logged body out of the water. Her head rolls back and her dead face smiles at me through dripping clown make-up. *How could you do this to her?* I demand, but he only mirrors her smile. I look back at her face, which lolls in the crook of my elbow, and see my own face, transplanted on her body.

I can't finish writing this dream. I wrap myself back in the tangled sheets and listen to the thunder growing ever nearer to the house.

Across the country from one another, Ma and Frank encounter identical beasts of solitude. Both lonely and heartbroken.

After a full day of teaching conservative, backwoods Vermont undergrads about polyamory and alternative relationship dynamics, Ma goes on a date. Unfortunately this man's online profile obscures his old age, his yellow teeth, and his bald spot, and he keeps steering the conversation back to his ex-wife.

After a full day of teaching lackadaisical sorority girls and football jocks about metered verse, Frank goes by herself to drink a half-priced martini in a bar that screens old movies on Tuesdays. This week is one of Frank's favorites: *Lolita*, 1962, but tonight Humbert Humbert fails to charm her. She wobbles home on her bike and enters the kitchen a bit peckish. Just a snack. She eats her roommate's entire chocolate bar with her foot propped in the fridge door. Dark chocolate with sea salt and almonds. She hides the wrapper in the bottom of the trash, more for her own peace of mind.

After Ma's disappointing date drops her off, she opens the freezer with a spoon in hand, knowing that her eighty-year-old roommate generally keeps a carton of ice cream on hand for her grandchildren's visits. Just a spoonful, a nightcap, to satisfy her sweet tooth. She eats the entire carton of Moose Tracks, chocolate fudge with peanut butter cups, with her elbow propped in the freezer door.

Big-Little Frank does her best to be big at all times. She has an agenda. She keeps a very extensive to-do list, or rather—*many* to-do lists, which proliferate in all of her pockets and turn to lint in the laundry. She gets up early and stays up late, running around town like a chicken with her head cut off. She tries to evenly distribute her energy towards professional, intellectual, social, and physical pursuits. Instead of balance, however, this distribution of energy often leads to excess. All of this excessive life-balancing leaves little time for frivolities like sleep or romance.

In Frank's hurry to get to class, she forgets to turn off the stove. She arrives huffing and puffing and sweating profusely and fumbles through her lesson.

When she returns home she can hear the smoke alarm from halfway down the block. The door is locked. Big-little Frank, where did you hide your key this time? It's not under the rug, it's not in the mailbox, it's not in the tomato plant. Finally, she reaches her hand around in the dark spiderwebbed shelves of the tool-shed, and finds her key. The entire house is a shade darker from the smoke, and her roommate's cast iron skillet spits flames from the stove.

Two boxes of baking soda later, Frank sits on the stoop, little. She feels small. Deflated. Limp, like the wet rag she used to beat down the flame. She calls Ma. Ma picks up immediately, as though she has been hovering over the phone for three weeks, waiting for her daughter to call.

"Momma!"

"My baby!"

"I-almost-burned-the-house-down-and-I'm-exhausted-and-my-students-think-I'm-an-idiot-and-I'm-lonely-and-so-tired-and-I-wish-you-were-here-to-hold-me-and-draw-me-a-bath-and-that-I-could-just-sleep-for-ever-but-that's-impossible-because-you're-so-far-away-and-I-have-so-much-to-do!"

Mom has joked for years that all the money she's saved from penny-pinching she's put towards a therapy fund for me. She finally urges me to schedule my first appointment. I am curious—perhaps my therapist can shed some light on my recent manic behavior. Already late, I wolf down my breakfast in a hurry. I rush and arrive sweating and with a stomach ache from worrying. In the waiting room, I sit next to two middle-aged women with bulging guts and faces slipping off their skulls. *In good company.* While I wait I read the pamphlets on the counter. Reiki. Acupuncture. Healing with Aromatherapy. I scan the shelves of natural deodorants, herbal teas, and essential oils. These objects make me nervous that I'm in the wrong office. I'm here for psychotherapy, not crystals and scents. Finally, the therapist calls me back into her office. I have already filled out paperwork with a cursory list of my problems, so I know that she holds in her hand the words "anxiety about the loss of time, inability to focus, inability to make decisions, possible depression, overeating, addiction to coffee and sugar, autoimmune disorders, stress..." Somewhere else in the paperwork I have written that my mother suffers from manic depression and may be a sex addict.

My therapist begins cheerfully enough, with small talk about the weather and what brought me to Iowa City. I want her to cut to the chase. While I'm in denial that anything is wrong, *I'm so functional! So accomplished! I have so many friends, see?* I also want verbal affirmation that I'm fucked up, and that I have battled enormous obstacles. I want both at once: a medal of honor for my hardships, and a reward for being so good and strong.

Instead, she asks the question that I dread, for there is no way to answer it simply: "Where are you from?" I offer my classic summary response, "I've moved a lot. West Coast, East Coast, mostly Vermont and Oregon, some California."

"But where were you born? Where did you most recently come from? You started off in Vermont, then moved to Oregon?" I shake my head and respond with a stronger tone of impatience than I mean to let on. *It's not so simple*, I think. *It's never so simple.*

"I was born in Salt Lake. My parents divorced when I was four, then my Mom moved to Santa Cruz. She's a professor, anthropology. I'm not sure what the actual custody situation was, I don't think it was 50-50, I think the judge was conservative and didn't like the fact that Mom had an affair, so I think my Dad had a greater portion of the custody. All of that's to say that I think my Mom took us to Santa Cruz without Dad's permission. He got us back after a year or so, somehow, then she moved back to Utah, then to Maine to teach at the University of Fort Kent. I think she kidnapped us that time too. We were there a year or two before Dad had the police put us on a plane back to Utah."

I watch her face for signals of empathy, some indication of her humanity. Instead, her face remains static, and she asks, "Were you aware of all of these struggles?"

"Vaguely aware, maybe I blocked out the specifics. Anyway, She moved back to Utah, bounced around some small towns like Alpine, Heber, back to Salt Lake. By that time, Dad married my stepmom and moved up to Portland. I was nine or ten, I think. He's been there ever since. Mom bounced around Utah a bit more, married my stepdad, and then followed Dad up to Portland to make logistics easier, but they didn't really like living in the same town, so when she got a job teaching in Vermont, she took it, and we followed. My sister and I, that is. It's confusing to explain, but we started off the school year with Dad and breaks with Mom, and at some point, around eight or nine, we switched to school years with Mom and breaks with Dad. So, even though Dad has lived in Portland for fourteen years or so, we don't fully know the town, I don't have school friends there. Anyway. I attended junior high school and high school in some small towns in Northeastern Vermont, then moved to Burlington for college. I lived there with my sister."

"How did she respond to all of this moving, and the divorce, and the kidnapping?"

"I'm not sure, to be honest. We've never talked about it. There were a few years in college when everyone, including her therapist, tried to convince her she was bipolar too, but she seems fine now, so maybe it was just her birth control pills."

My therapist takes a moment to take a few notes. She frowns as she scribbles, and the source of her frown remains a mystery to me. She seems to be playing this safe, and won't allow me the affirmation I'm seeking. I want her to say, "my goodness, you've had a crazy childhood! I'm impressed that you've lived through such adventures and are so perfectly normal now—a testament to your strength!" Instead, she says in a neutral tone,

"You must have grown up quickly."

"Well put. You hit it on the nail," I said, almost cheerfully, as though we had discovered the source of all of my problems. I don't know what game I'm trying to play with her—I want her sympathy, but also I want her to confirm that I'm completely stable and healthy. I want her to be on my team, but it's seeming more difficult to show her how capable and perceptive I am. I'm crossing my wires. I'm offering her accidental flashes of my inner chaos. She seems unfazed by the edge in my voice. I begin to tear up and grab a wad of tissues.

"Yeah, I remember when it hit me that Mom wasn't the ultimate authority, the trustworthy parent, the model for morality and behavior. Mom always told us about her difficulty with money. Paying the bills, the year she didn't have insurance and had her appendix taken out for $15,000, and so on. Her mom was a baby of the Great Depression, and passed on her thrift to Mom, an extreme penny-pinching tendency. Soon after we moved to Vermont and Mom took on a new mortgage for a house too large for her budget, she whimsically proposed one day that she might get a motorcycle. That's when I realized that some aspects of my maturity surpassed my own mother's—that was hard. Still is, but I guess I'm used to it."

"You became a 'parentalized child' from a young age."

"Interesting."

She looked me in the eye for a bit too long, and I thought she may be practicing some unspoken hypnotism or telepathy. She finally breaks the silence.

"How does all of this make you feel? Do you ever allow yourself to be sad?"

"Of course, especially recently, but then it gets me thinking that I'm depressed and that makes me even more sad and it feels like a waste of time. Depression runs in my family. All of my uncles and aunts are depressed. My mom tells me half-jokingly all the time things like, 'you're the only happy one in the family, we're just counting down the days until you become one of us,' so that when I go through periods of darkness I feel like I'm slipping into the patterns of my family's mental illness. It scares the hell out of me."

"That must be really hard."

My therapist looks at her watch. "Unfortunately, we're out of time, and we haven't yet addressed your overeating and addiction to coffee, chocolate, and alcohol. We'll pick up where we left off in the next session. Do you have any questions?"

"Sorry to unload so much in one session..."

"Don't worry, you have a lot that you felt you needed to say."

I don't know how to interpret this comment. She walks me to the lobby so that I can give the receptionist my copay, and she returns to her office. While I wait for the receptionist to process my bill, I flip through a stack of Psychology Today magazines. There's an article called "Hypomania vs. Manic-Depression, What's the Difference?" I slip the magazine into my backpack.

I wait until I'm outside to skim through the article, which quotes the DSM, or the *Diagnostic and Statistical Manual of Mental Disorders*. Apparently, there's a milder version of manic depression called "bipolar II disorder." The magazine includes contrasting lists of symptoms of the two disorders. I make a mental checklist of those that apply to me and a parallel checklist of those that apply to Mom. It's too much to take in while standing, so I pop into a nearby cafe and order an enormous chocolate cookie and a coffee, even though I just had breakfast and my stomach feels bloated with stress. I curse myself for my sugar addiction, take a messy bite, and nearly gag on the cookie when I read, "Excessive involvement in pleasurable activities that have a high potential for painful consequences, such as binge eating, unrestrained buying sprees, or sexual indiscretions." I scowl at my cookie and push it across the table.

I Google "hypomania" for more information. This illness is diagnosed as "recurrent depression accompanied by hypomanic episodes." Descriptions of these episodes hit disturbingly close to home. I translate the symptoms into my own behavior: irrational energetic bursts, egoism, lack of sleep, inane chatter, flights of ideas, racing thoughts, distractibility to external stimuli, increase in goal-oriented activity.

I think of my never-ending and ever-expanding to-do lists. I can picture my desk at home piled high with towers of papers, journals, books, and drawings. I see my hands in perpetual motion, always doodling, fiddling, drumming on the desk, taking notes. My mouth must be active at all times—talking, chewing gum, eating, slurping, sipping. I have an addictive personality: coffee, chocolate, alcohol, exercise. I am always either desperately lonely or juggling lovers. My calendar bursts with overlapping social commitments. I simultaneously despise my body and move through the world with a sense of grandiosity. I can't sit still.

I chug my entire sixteen ounce coffee, shove the cookie into my mouth, exit the cafe, and call my mother. Maybe she can act as my therapy interpreter, my secondary session. She can fill in where the therapist was too vague, too cold and dispassionate. I avoid mention of the hypomania and guilt and worry and instead complain about my therapist's indifferent countenance. I don't mention my self-diagnosis of hypomania.

She calms me down, gives me the verbal affection that I need, and asks about my work. I tell her I'm still writing about her, and she gives me permission to write about her recent pubic hair removal laser treatment.

"It looks like I contracted some horrible, mysterious rash down there. Everywhere. I've swelled up like some venereal lobster. I'm too embarrassed, I cancelled all my dates for the week."

the CAVE

If Ma and Frank were classical heroes or if they fit more perfectly into universal symbology, here they would encounter a dragon. Or, they would fly up into the sun with makeshift wings, and their waxed feathers would melt into the sea. Instead, they encounter an old, fat, toothless man in the woods and poison oak. Frank, the hero-trickster, enters the dark cave of her psyche, embraces the discomfort therein, and interrogates the unknown of her interiority. She must kill her infantile attachment to Ma and initiate a more mature and productive life. Here in the cave she finds an animal guardian: a rabbit, who should help her cope with her own insecurities, but instead the rabbit reminds her of her own weakness. This sad, shivering creature is a reflection of Frank's vulnerability. Frank now feels that she must save the rabbit in order to save herself. Her task is to write herself out of the cave of her own mind.

Ma pays Frank a spontaneous visit. She buys a flight to Iowa without asking about Frank's schedule. Frank glances at her phone during a morning seminar to find Ma's text, "I'm on my way to visit you, can you pick me up from the airport at noon?" Frank bristles and panics—this is Ma at her shape-shifting peak. This is wild Ma, young and impulsive Ma. This is not-to-be-relied-upon-Ma.

These are Frank's thoughts as she drives to the airport, but as she pulls up to see Ma waving both her arms from the curb, Frank becomes a wet sponge. She, wet-sponge Frank, melts into Ma's breasts and salts the skin of Ma's neck.

Frank takes Ma to a swimming hole, where fat, violent catfish leap in a shallow bay. The fish are either fighting or mating, but either action causes quite a ruckus in the water.

Ma reclines in a patch of prairie grass, and Frank lies across her like a heavy, sweaty pillow. Here, in this muddy pretzel knot, all mother-daughter tension melts, loosening the skin between Frank's eyebrows and under her shoulder blades, unknotting her belly. She floats in Ma's arms and is little again. Little Frank and her Ma.

Back on shore, they squat to pee. Unfortunately, their chosen squatting ground turns out to be a patch of poison oak. They drive to a nearby farmhouse where

Ma asks a toothless, bloated fellow if they might borrow his hose and a bar of soap.

"You sisters?"

"No. We got into some poison oak, do you have soap?"

"Might. I have kittens, d'you wanna take a look?"

"No, but we would appreciate some soap and a hose. Thank you."

When the man isn't looking, they both strip down and help each other rinse away the oils of poison oak. The man with no teeth watches this strange couple from the garden. Lovers? Sisters? They dance over the hose coiled at their feet as though it were a vanquished serpent. They stand goose-pimpled, raw from scrubbing, naked by the side of the road, laughing and crying. They laugh-cry away this preposterous year of travel, divorce, and illness. They laugh-cry that at twenty-five and fifty, they could be sisters. They laugh-cry that Ma is such a kid, and Frank is so old. They laugh-cry with the relief of their mutual affection. Ma and Frank, so little, so big.

Frank takes Ma to her favorite brunch spot. It's a little outside of town, out in the country, and all the eggs and vegetables and meat are "organic, sustainable, supplied by nearby farms, all that jazz," she tells Ma as they settle into a booth by the window, but she can tell that Ma isn't listening—her attention has already been diverted to the spectacle of the waiter. To Frank, he looks a bit short, squat, and red in the face, but the way Ma is ogling him, there must be some sex appeal, maybe in the tight-ish butt that peeks over his leather belt or the muscles that bulge through the arms of his black t-shirt as he carries around a carafe of coffee. Ma orders a tall Bloody Mary and stuffs the glass with extra olives and horseradish and Frank orders their favorite standby: Eggs Benedict, but the pleasure and attention of this dish are overshadowed by Ma's new game.

"Should I ask for his number?"

Frank shrugs and spreads egg yolk on her half of the biscuit, doing her best to give the yolk her full attention. Eggs are her favorite food, and these eggs—plucked from beneath a hen's bum this very morning—have particularly vibrant yolks. Ma hasn't moved on from her schoolgirl crush.

"Maybe I'll write a little note on a napkin or the receipt. What should I say?"

"I've got the munchies! My sweet tooth is acting up. Where's the cake? The ice cream? Anyone got a secret stash of chocolate somewhere? I must be *so high*. Am I the only one feeling this good?"

Frank looks straight ahead. She will not, *must not* acknowledge Ma's comment. She rolls her eyes to signal to her friends that she is embarrassed. She knows her Ma is silly and tries to laugh a little bit, but her mouth can only form a grimace. Frank doesn't give a damn about Nicolette or her theatrical pursuits, but she must not let Ma take over. So she asks,

What were you saying Nicolette?"

Nicolette continues to describe her new role. She must learn to master the accent of a Southern Belle. She must dye her hair. The bong goes around the table again, and when it arrives in Ma's hands, just as she lifts the glass to her wet, slippery lips, Frank hisses from behind her palm,

Take it easy."

Lips retreat in on themselves like the lips of the toothless old man from their poison oak disaster. Her lips collapse inwards into the black hole of a scowl. Ma has stolen Nicolette's role as a heartbroken Does Frank see her drama? Frank sees. Ma jumps up, knocking her plate off the table. The steak falls to Ma's white blouse and leaves a bloody red-meat stain over her left breast. The wet stain illuminates the now very visible absence of Ma's bra.

98

Frank shrugs again. She tries to engage Ma in various conversations, but it's like trying to lead a dog away from a squirrel. She tries:

"How do you handle slacker undergrad students when you teach?"

"Is your menstrual cycle synced up with the moon?"

"What did you read on your train ride across Russia when you were nineteen?"

By the time they get their check, Ma has set up a date.

Frank feels little again. She knows that she is acting up, on the verge of throwing a tantrum, like her toddler self, but she doesn't know why. Shame for a loose Ma? Fear that Ma cares more about men than about Frank? Boredom in the monotony of Ma's man-driven talk and gaze? Perhaps she is protecting Ma from future heartbreak, from divorce #3. Maybe she's tired of guiding Ma through the up and down arc and plummet of so many relationships. Of being the guidance-counsellor-best-friend-daughter-mother-cheering-squad-safety-net for Ma's continual sexual pursuits. Maybe Frank's jealous because she sleeps alone and nobody ever asks her out for drinks or dinner or sleepovers. Maybe she's angry at Ma for being healthy and hot while Frank is the only one in the family with an ill body. A reptile freak with dragon-scale skin.

95

Frank brings Ma along to a dinner party. Th
everything comes apart. The host of the p;
the guests are Frank's age, twenty
students and baristas and the like, but M;
She cracks sex jokes as the host flips s
grill. She rambles on and on about h
Tinder, Twitter, polyamory, craft beer.
so fun, so young, so hip! Frank steps ir
bathroom and hopes that Ma doesn't
the host while she's away.

When she returns, Ma is sucking (
table. This is not Frank's type of p;
had a few beers, but this only acce
Ma giggles, coughs, sucks, giggl
chokes, coughs, laughs. Ma is fu
red in the face, red all over: her
lipsticked lips, the steak on |
requested "rare, like a slice righ
red of all is Ma's tongue, lol'
mouth.

Whenever Ma cracks a joke i
rolls her eyes and looks awa
the guests—Nicolette, a div
her lead role in a local
Named Desire. A fam
handpicked Nicolette for
Ma interrupts this
announcement,

Ni
m
Sh
tab
Ma
fror

"Tak

Ma's
tooth
lips c
Now M
diva.
stands
flips on
brown
accentu

Frank shrugs again. She tries to engage Ma in various conversations, but it's like trying to lead a dog away from a squirrel. She tries:

"How do you handle slacker undergrad students when you teach?"

"Is your menstrual cycle synced up with the moon?"

"What did you read on your train ride across Russia when you were nineteen?"

By the time they get their check, Ma has set up a date.

Frank feels little again. She knows that she is acting up, on the verge of throwing a tantrum, like her toddler self, but she doesn't know why. Shame for a loose Ma? Fear that Ma cares more about men than about Frank? Boredom in the monotony of Ma's man-driven talk and gaze? Perhaps she is protecting Ma from future heartbreak, from divorce #3. Maybe she's tired of guiding Ma through the up and down arc and plummet of so many relationships. Of being the guidance-counsellor-best-friend-daughter-mother-cheering-squad-safety-net for Ma's continual sexual pursuits. Maybe Frank's jealous because she sleeps alone and nobody ever asks her out for drinks or dinner or sleepovers. Maybe she's angry at Ma for being healthy and hot while Frank is the only one in the family with an ill body. A reptile freak with dragon-scale skin.

Frank brings Ma along to a dinner party. This is when everything comes apart. The host of the party and all the guests are Frank's age, twenty-something students and baristas and the like, but Ma fits right in. She cracks sex jokes as the host flips steaks on the grill. She rambles on and on about hip topics like Tinder, Twitter, polyamory, craft beer. She is on fire, so fun, so young, so hip! Frank steps inside to use the bathroom and hopes that Ma doesn't make a pass at the host while she's away.

When she returns, Ma is sucking on a bong at the table. This is not Frank's type of party. Sure, Frank's had a few beers, but this only accentuates her shame. Ma giggles, coughs, sucks, giggles, coughs, laughs, chokes, coughs, laughs. Ma is fun, see Ma run! Ma is red in the face, red all over: her bloodshot eyes, her lipsticked lips, the steak on her plate, which she requested "rare, like a slice right outta the cow." Most red of all is Ma's tongue, lolling around in her big mouth.

Whenever Ma cracks a joke in Frank's direction, Frank rolls her eyes and looks away. Across the table, one of the guests—Nicolette, a diva of the theater—describes her lead role in a local production of A Streetcar Named Desire. A famous indie film director handpicked Nicolette for his new, secret film project. Ma interrupts this story with an important announcement,

"I've got the munchies! My sweet tooth is acting up. Where's the cake? The ice cream? Anyone got a secret stash of chocolate somewhere? I must be *so high*. Am I the only one feeling this good?"

Frank looks straight ahead. She will not, *must not* acknowledge Ma's comment. She rolls her eyes to signal to her friends that she is embarrassed. She knows her Ma is silly and tries to laugh a little bit, but her mouth can only form a grimace. Frank doesn't give a damn about Nicolette or her theatrical pursuits, but she must not let Ma take over. So she asks,

"What were you saying Nicolette?"

Nicolette continues to describe her new role. She must learn to master the accent of a Southern Belle. She must dye her hair. The bong goes around the table again, and when it arrives in Ma's hands, just as Ma lifts the glass to her wet, slippery lips, Frank hisses from behind her palm,

"Take it easy."

Ma's lips retreat in on themselves like the lips of the toothless old man from their poison oak disaster. Her lips collapse inwards into the black hole of a scowl. Now Ma has stolen Nicolette's role as a heartbroken diva. Does Frank see her drama? Frank sees. Ma stands up, knocking her plate off the table. The steak flips onto Ma's white blouse and leaves a bloody red-brown stain over her left breast. The wet stain accentuates the now very visible absence of Ma's bra.